PIANO · VOCAL · GUITAR

2nd Edition

ULTIMATE

MOVIE MUSIC

70 MEMORABLE HITS

T0053168

ISBN-13: 978-0-7935-7675-3
ISBN-10: 0-7935-7675-X

HAL • LEONARD®
CORPORATION
7777 W. BLUEMOUND RD. P.O. BOX 13819 MILWAUKEE, WI 53213

Visit Hal Leonard Online at
www.halleonard.com

CONTENTS

4	All the Way	The Joker Is Wild (1957)
6	Big Spender	Sweet Charity (1969)
9	Breakaway	The Princess Diaries 2: Royal Engagement (2004)
16	Can You Feel the Love Tonight	The Lion King (1994)
20	Can't Help Falling in Love	Blue Hawaii (1962)
24	Cavatina	The Deer Hunter (1978)
28	Change the World	Phenomenon (1996)
34	Chariots of Fire	Chariots of Fire (1981)
44	Cinema Paradiso	Cinema Paradiso (1989)
37	Colors of the Wind	Pocahontas (1995)
46	Cruella De Vil	101 Dalmatians (1996)
52	Do You Know Where You're Going To?	Mahogany (1976)
58	Driving Miss Daisy	Driving Miss Daisy (1989)
62	Easter Parade	Easter Parade (1948)
66	Theme from E.T.	E.T. (The Extra-Terrestrial) (1982)
72	Love Theme from "Flashdance"	Flashdance (1983)
76	Forrest Gump – Main Title	Forrest Gump (1994)
80	The Godfather Waltz	The Godfather (1972)
84	High Noon (Do Not Forsake Me)	High Noon (1952)
90	I Believe in You and Me	The Preacher's Wife (1996)
97	I Finally Found Someone	The Mirror Has Two Faces (1996)
104	I Walk the Line	I Walk the Line (2005)
106	I Will Always Love You	The Bodyguard (1992)
118	I Will Follow Him	Sister Act (1992)
122	If I Were a Rich Man	Fiddler on the Roof (1971)
130	Il Postino (The Postman)	Il Postino (1994)
111	Journey to the Past	Anastasia (1997)
134	The Last Time I Felt Like This	Same Time, Next Year (1978)
138	Legends of the Fall	Legends of the Fall (1994)
144	Let the River Run	Working Girl (1988)
150	Love Me Tender	Love Me Tender (1956)
152	The Man from Snowy River (Main Title Theme)	The Man from Snowy River (1982)
141	Midnight Cowboy	Midnight Cowboy (1969)
154	Moon River	Breakfast at Tiffany's (1961)
157	The Nearness of You	Romance in the Dark (1940)

162	Nine to Five	Nine to Five (1980)
166	No Two People	Hans Christian Andersen (1952)
176	The Odd Couple	The Odd Couple (1968)
171	On Golden Pond	On Golden Pond (1981)
180	One Tin Soldier	Billy Jack (1971)
183	Theme from "Ordinary People"	Ordinary People (1980)
186	I Had a Farm in Africa (Main Theme)	Out of Africa (1985)
190	The Rainbow Connection	The Muppet Movie (1979)
195	Raindrops Keep Fallin' on My Head	Butch Cassidy and the Sundance Kid (1969)
198	Say You, Say Me	White Nights (1985)
208	Theme from "Schindler's List"	Schindler's List (1993)
210	Sea of Love	Sea of Love (1989)
203	Seasons of Love	Rent (2005)
214	Theme from Shaft	Shaft (1971)
222	Somewhere in Time	Somewhere in Time (1980)
219	Somewhere, My Love	Doctor Zhivago (1965)
224	A Spoonful of Sugar	Mary Poppins (1964)
232	Love Theme from "St. Elmo's Fire"	St. Elmo's Fire (1985)
227	Stayin' Alive	Saturday Night Fever (1977)
234	Stormy Weather	Stormy Weather (1943)
238	The Stripper	The Stripper (1963)
250	Tammy	Tammy and the Bachelor (1957)
252	Taxi Driver	Taxi Driver (1976)
241	Teacher's Pet	Teacher's Pet (1958)
254	Theme from "Terms of Endearment"	Terms of Endearment (1983)
260	That Thing You Do!	That Thing You Do! (1996)
264	(I've Had) The Time of My Life	Dirty Dancing (1987)
274	To Sir, With Love	To Sir, With Love (1967)
277	Top Hat, White Tie and Tails	Top Hat (1935)
282	Viva Las Vegas	Viva Las Vegas (1963)
288	The Way We Were	The Way We Were (1973)
291	When I Fall in Love	Sleepless in Seattle (1993)
294	Where Is Your Heart	Moulin Rouge (1952)
297	You Must Love Me	Evita (1996)
300	Young at Heart	Young at Heart (1954)

ALL THE WAY

from THE JOKER IS WILD

Words by SAMMY CAHN
Music by JAMES VAN HEUSEN

When some-bod-y loves you, it's no good un-less he loves you all the
When some-bod-y needs you, it's no good un-less she needs you all the

way.
way.

Hap-py to be near you, when you need some-one to cheer you
Thru the good or lean years and for all the in-be-tween years,

all the way.
come what may.

Tall-er _____ than the tall-est tree is,
Who knows _____ where the road will lead us,

BIG SPENDER
from SWEET CHARITY

Words by DOROTHY FIELDS
Music by CY COLEMAN

The min-ute you walked in the joint, I could see you were a man of dis-tinc-tion, a real big spend-er, good look-ing, so re-fined. Say, would-n't you like to know what's go-ing on in my mind? So let me get right to the point,

BREAKAWAY

from THE PRINCESS DIARIES 2: ROYAL ENGAGEMENT

Words and Music by BRIDGET BENENATE,
AVRIL LAVIGNE and MATTHEW GERRARD

Grew up in a small town and when the rain would fall down,

I'd just stare out my win - dow. Dream-in' of what could be

and if I'd end up hap - py. I would pray.

Try - ing hard to reach out but when I tried to speak out,
Wan - na feel the warm breeze. Sleep un - der a palm tree.

CAN YOU FEEL THE LOVE TONIGHT

from Walt Disney Pictures' THE LION KING

Music by ELTON JOHN
Lyrics by TIM RICE

CAN'T HELP FALLING IN LOVE

from the Paramount Picture BLUE HAWAII

Words and Music by GEORGE DAVID WEISS,
HUGO PERETTI and LUIGI CREATORE

Slowly, steadily

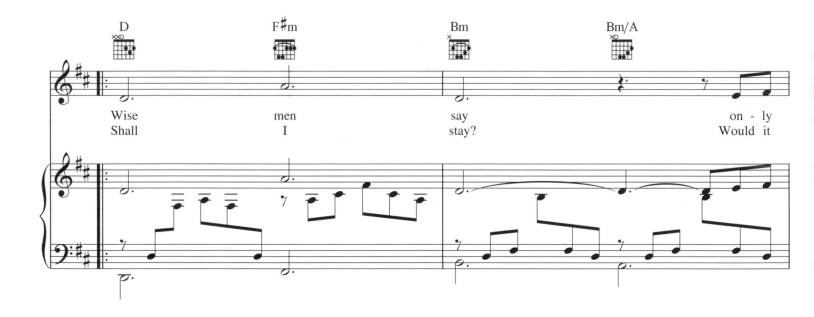

Wise   men   say   on - ly
Shall   I   stay?   Would it

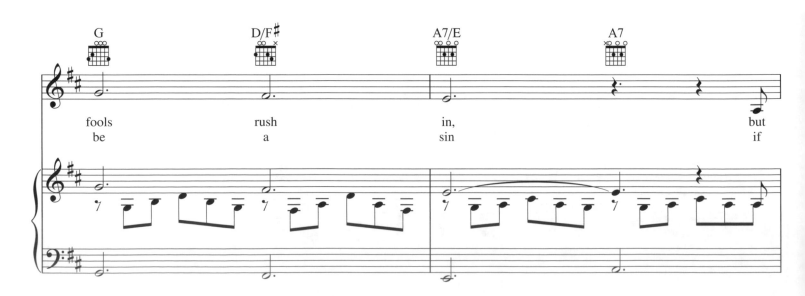

fools   rush   in,   but
be   a   sin   if

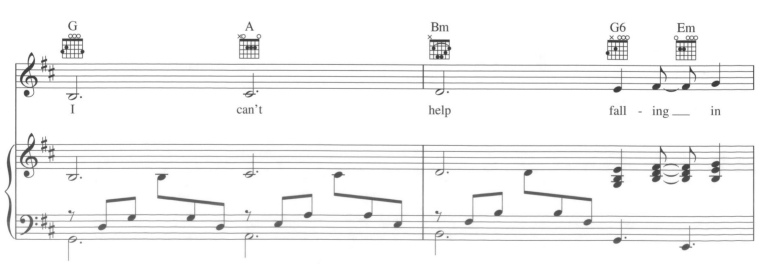

F#m B7 Em A7

some things _ are _ meant to be.

D F#m Bm

Take my hand, take my

G D/F# A7/E A7

whole life too, for

G A Bm G6 Em

I can't help fall - ing _ in

CAVATINA

from the Universal Pictures and EMI Films Presentation THE DEER HUNTER

By STANLEY MYERS

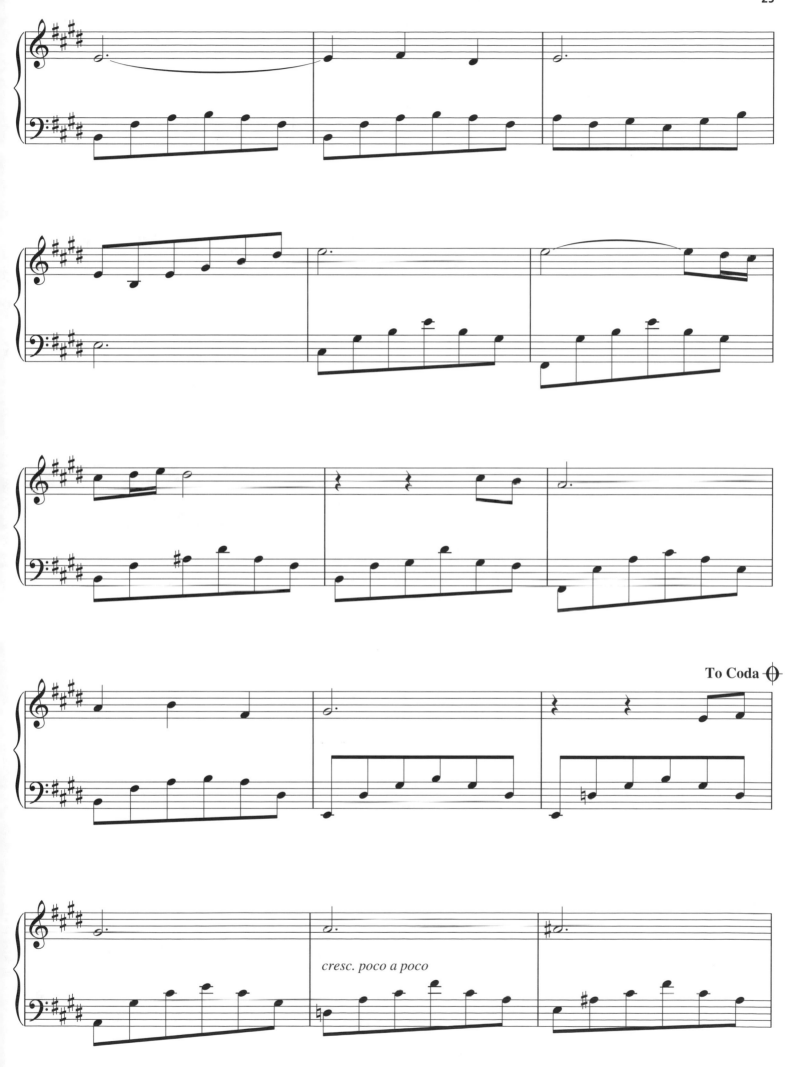

To Coda ⊕

cresc. poco a poco

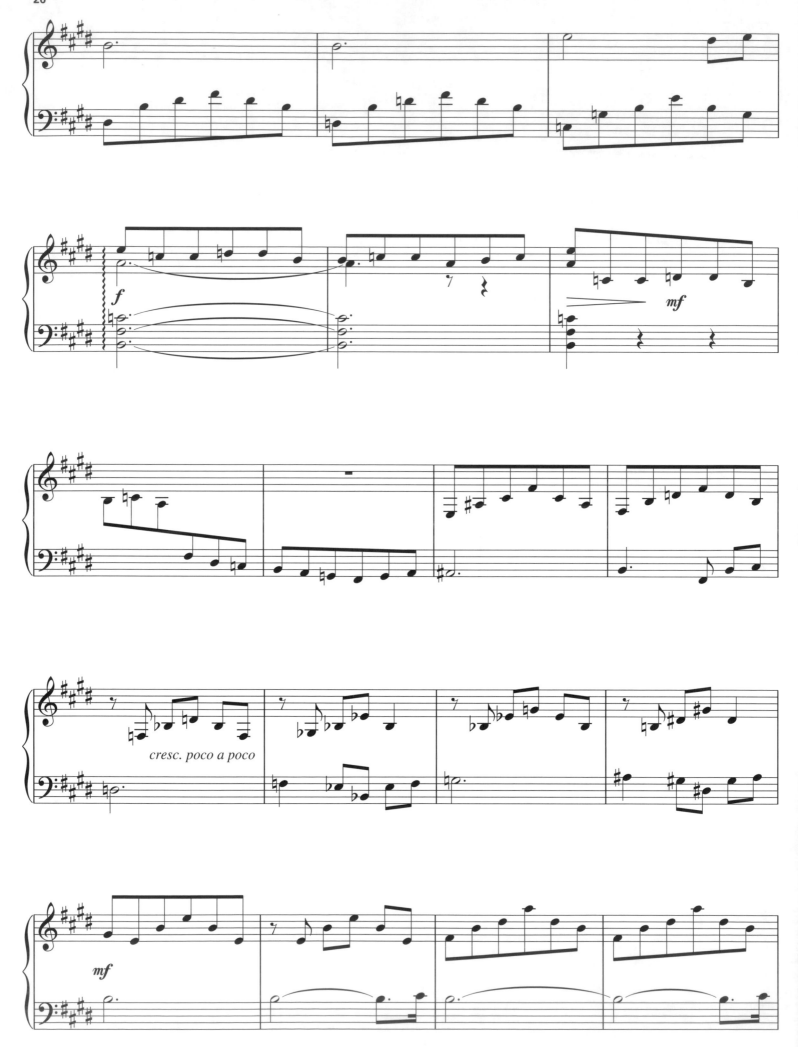

CHANGE THE WORLD

featured on the Motion Picture Soundtrack PHENOMENON

Words and Music by WAYNE KIRKPATRICK,
GORDON KENNEDY and TOMMY SIMS

CHARIOTS OF FIRE

from CHARIOTS OF FIRE

Music by VANGELIS

Moderately

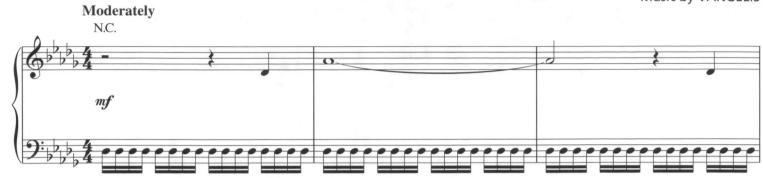

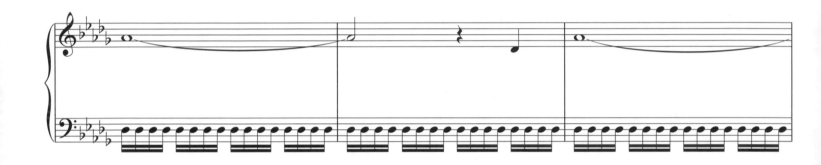

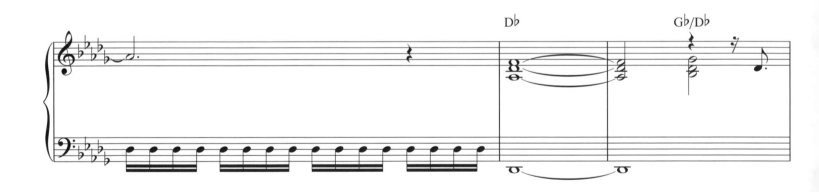

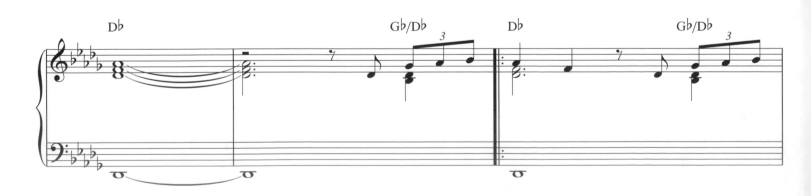

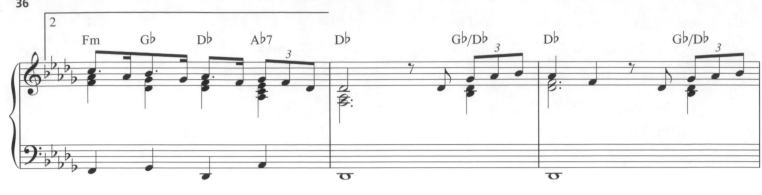

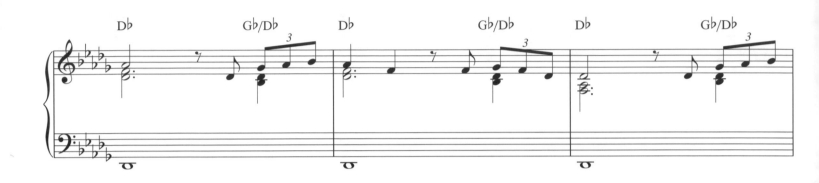

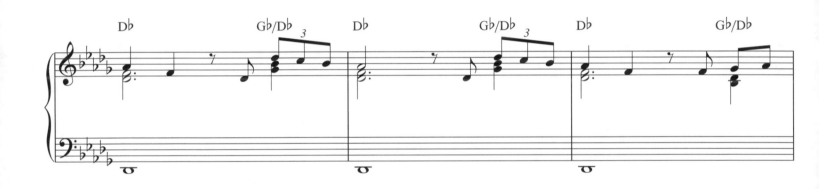

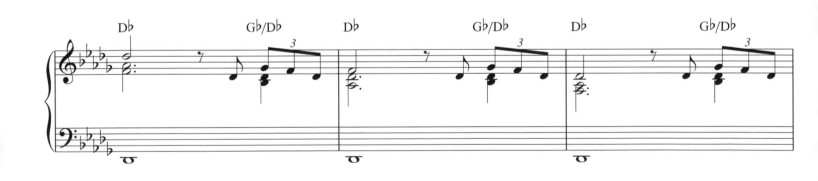

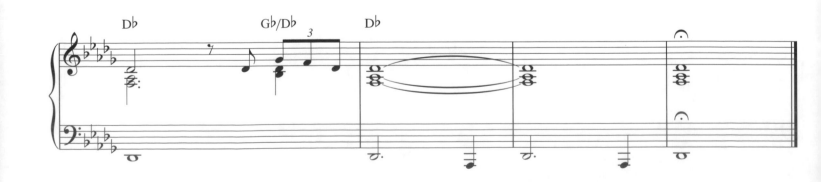

COLORS OF THE WIND

from Walt Disney's POCAHONTAS

Music by ALAN MENKEN
Lyrics by STEPHEN SCHWARTZ

Deliberately

think I'm an ig-no-rant sav-age, and you've been so man-y plac-es, I guess it must be so. But

Freely

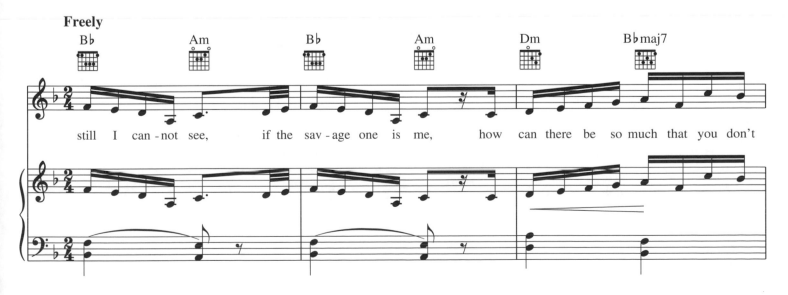

still I can-not see, if the sav-age one is me, how can there be so much that you don't

CINEMA PARADISO

from CINEMA PARADISO

Music by ENNIO MORRICONE

Simply, with feeling

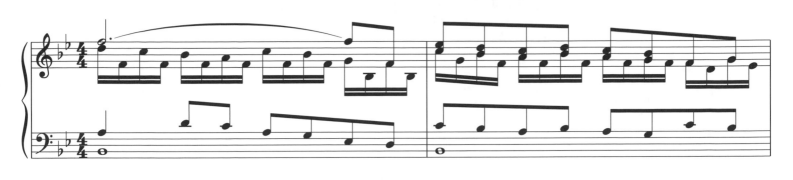

CRUELLA DE VIL

from Walt Disney's 101 DALMATIANS

Words and Music by
MEL LEVEN

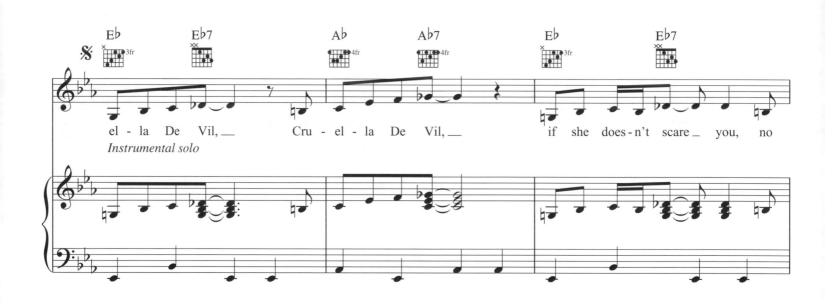

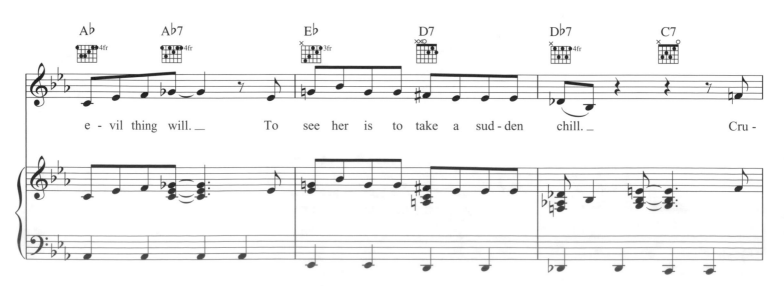

Cru - el - la _____ De Vil.

Spoken: So evil,
And like nothin' you
I need to mention she's got some

even her hair's two-faced.
ever seen, she's the dean of mean.
dog-gone bad intentions.

(Spoken:) I mean, let's face it, a person like her could really ruin your whole day.

DO YOU KNOW WHERE YOU'RE GOING TO?

Theme from MAHOGANY

Words by GERRY GOFFIN
Music by MIKE MASSER

DRIVING MISS DAISY

from DRIVING MISS DAISY

By HANS ZIMMER

Moderately

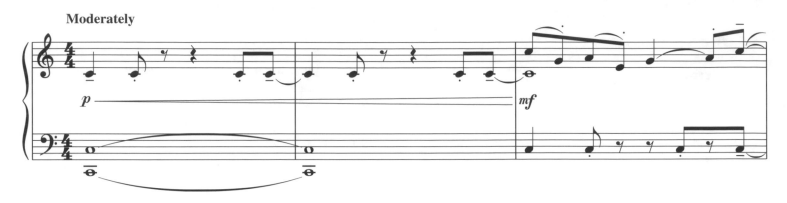

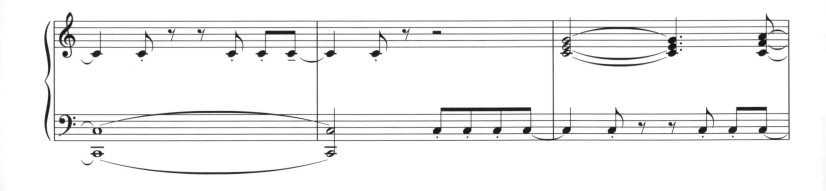

EASTER PARADE

featured in the Motion Picture Irving Berlin's EASTER PARADE

Words and Music by
IRVING BERLIN

Lyrics:

Nev-er saw you look quite so pret-ty be-fore. ___

___ Nev-er saw you dressed quite so love-ly,what's more ___

64

la - dy in the Eas - ter pa - rade. {I'll / You'll} be all in

clo - ver and when they look {you / me} o - ver {I'll / you'll} be the proud - est

fel - low in the Eas - ter pa - rade. On the

Av - e - nue, Fifth Av - e - nue,

THEME FROM E.T.
(The Extra-Terrestrial)
from the Universal Picture E.T. (THE EXTRA-TERRESTRIAL)

Music by JOHN WILLIAMS

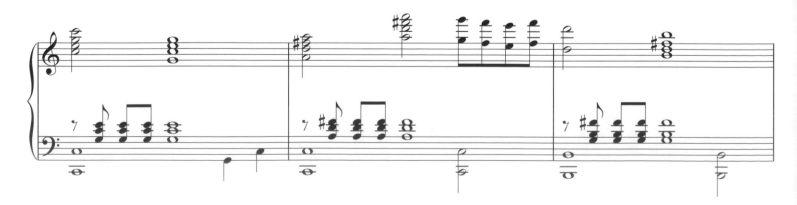

LOVE THEME FROM "FLASHDANCE"

from the Paramount Picture FLASHDANCE

Music by GIORGIO MORODER

Moderately slow

mf

With pedal

FORREST GUMP – MAIN TITLE
(Feather Theme)
from the Paramount Motion Picture FORREST GUMP

Music by ALAN SILVESTRI

8va ----------

f

(lightly)

THE GODFATHER WALTZ

from the Paramount Pictures THE GODFATHER, GODFATHER II, and GODFATHER III

By NINO ROTA

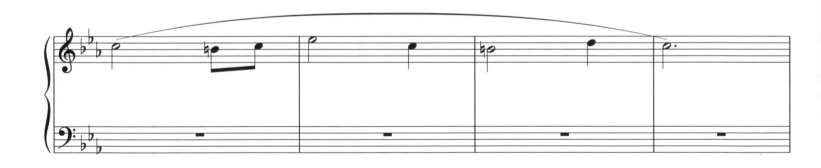

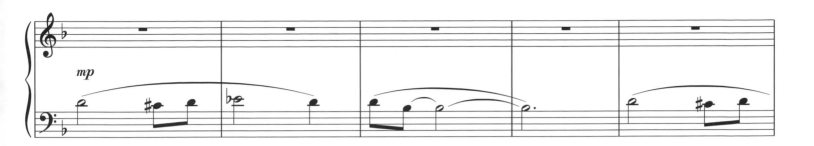

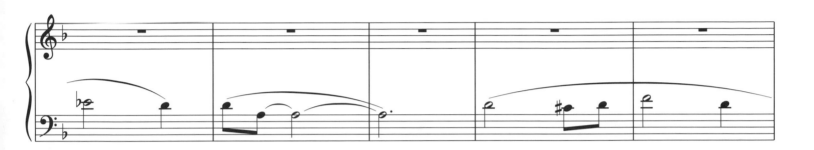

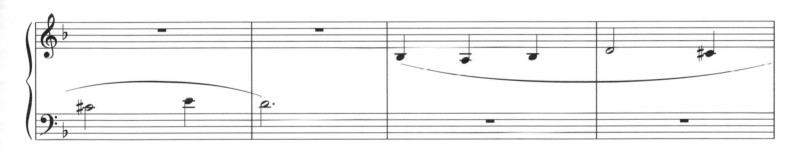

Moderately slow

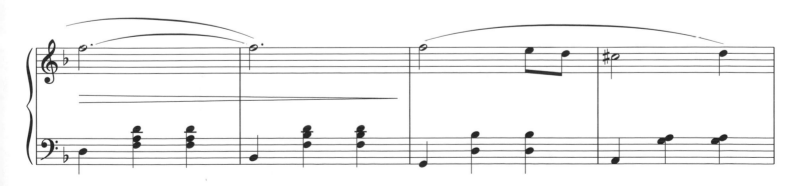

HIGH NOON
(Do Not Forsake Me)
from HIGH NOON

Words and Music by DIMITRI TIOMKIN
and NED WASHINGTON

I BELIEVE IN YOU AND ME

from the Touchstone Motion Picture THE PREACHER'S WIFE

Words and Music by DAVID WOLFERT
and SANDY LINZER

can't you see _____ that I be-lieve _ in you _____ and me.

May - be I'm a fool _____ to feel the way _ I do. _____

I would play _____ the fool for-ev - er _____ just to be with you _____ for-ev - er. _____

I FINALLY FOUND SOMEONE

from THE MIRROR HAS TWO FACES

Words and Music by BARBRA STREISAND,
MARVIN HAMLISCH, ROBERT LANGE
and BRYAN ADAMS

Male: I fi-n'lly found some-one who knocks me off my feet.

I fi-n'lly found the one ___ that makes me feel com-plete.

Female: It start-ed o-ver cof-fee. We start-ed out as friends.

ev - er I do, _____ *Male:* it's just got to be you. _____ *Both:* My

life has just be - gun. I fi - n'lly found some - one. _____

Male: Did I keep you wait - ing? I a - pol - o - gize. _____

Female: I did - n't mind. _____ Ba - by, that's fine. _____

I WALK THE LINE

Words and Music by
JOHN R. CASH

Additional Lyrics

3. As sure as night is dark and day is light,
   I keep you on my mind both day and night.
   And happiness I've known proves that it's right.
   Because you're mine I walk the line.

4. You've got a way to keep me on your side.
   You give me cause for love that I can't hide.
   For you I know I'd even try to turn the tide.
   Because you're mine I walk the line.

5. I keep a close watch on this heart of mine.
   I keep my eyes wide open all the time.
   I keep the ends out for the tie that binds.
   Because you're mine I walk the line.

I WILL ALWAYS LOVE YOU

from THE BODYGUARD

Words and Music by
DOLLY PARTON

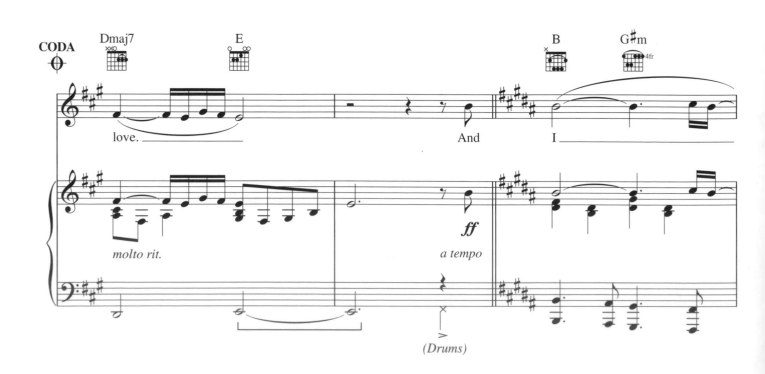

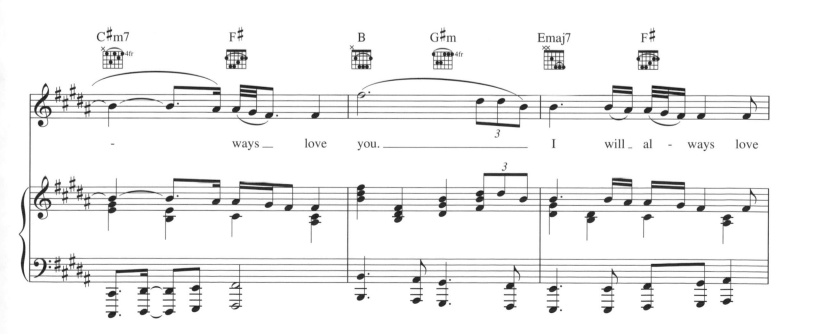

Additional Lyrics

3. I hope life treats you kind.
   And I hope you have all you've dreamed of.
   And I wish to you, joy and happiness.
   But above all this, I wish you love.

JOURNEY TO THE PAST

from the Twentieth Century Fox Motion Picture ANASTASIA

Words and Music by LYNN AHRENS
and STEPHEN FLAHERTY

Moderately ♩ = 88

Bm7   Em7

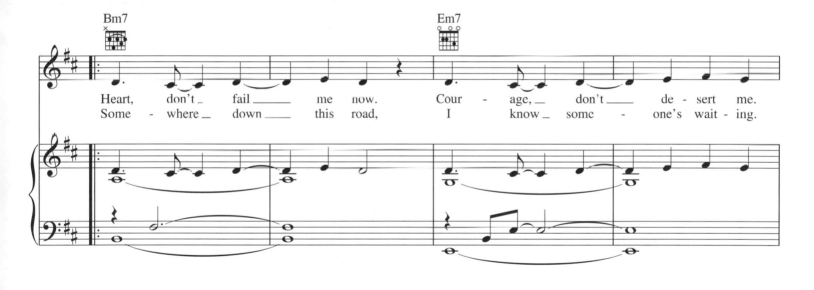

Heart, don't fail me now. Courage, don't desert me.
Somewhere down this road, I know someone's waiting.

Bm7   Em7

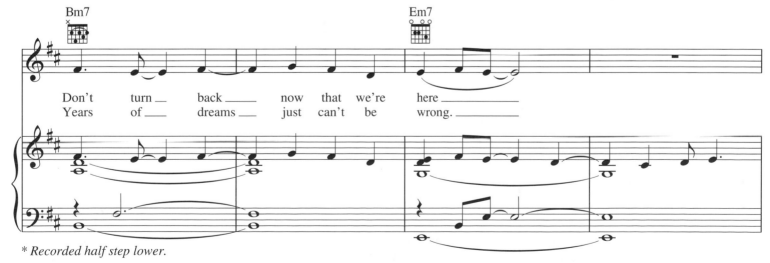

Don't turn back now that we're here
Years of dreams just can't be wrong.

* Recorded half step lower.

I WILL FOLLOW HIM
(I Will Follow You)
featured in the Motion Picture SISTER ACT

English Words by NORMAN GIMBEL and ARTHUR ALTMAN
French Words by JACQUES PLANTE
Music by J.W. STOLE and DEL ROMA

Moderately, with a beat

I will fol-low him, _____ fol-low him wher-ev-er he may go. _____ There is-n't an o-cean too deep, a moun-tain so high it can keep me a-

IF I WERE A RICH MAN

from the Musical FIDDLER ON THE ROOF

Words by SHELDON HARNICK
Music by JERRY BOCK

Oy! What a hap-py mood she's in. Scream-ing at the ser-vants day and

Rubato

night. The most im-por-tant men in town will come to fawn on ___ me;

they will ask me to ad-vise them, like Sol-o-mon the wise. "If you

please, Reb Tev-ye, par-don me, Reb Tev-ye." Pos-ing prob-lems what would cross a rab-bi's eyes.

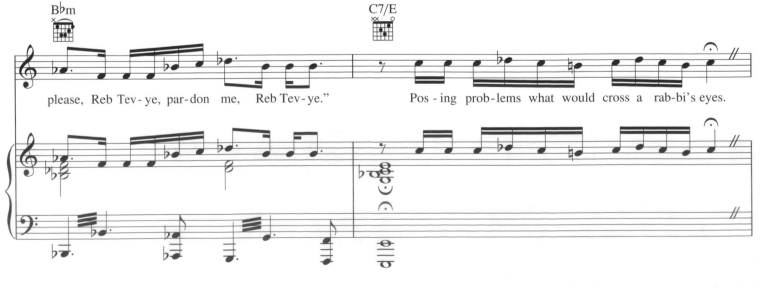

man. Would-n't have to work hard, dai-dle, dee-dle, dai-dle, dig-guh, dig-guh, dee-dle, dai-dle,

Rubato

dum. Lord, who make the li-on and the lamb, you de-creed I

should be what I am. Would it spoil some vast e-ter-nal plan if I were a wealth-y

man? _____

IL POSTINO
(The Postman)
from IL POSTINO

Music by LUIS BACALOV

Moderato

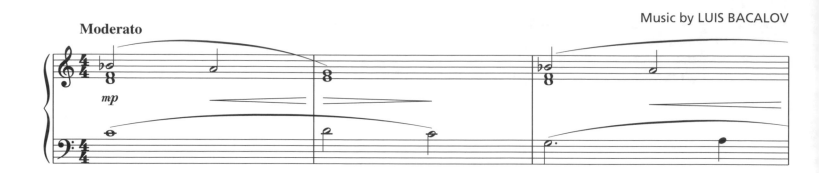

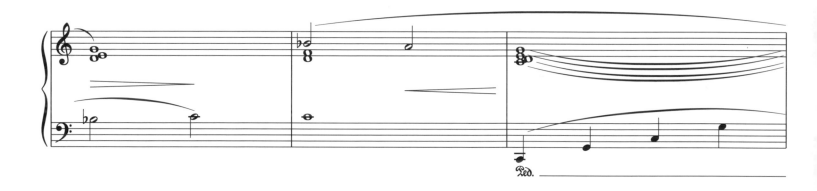

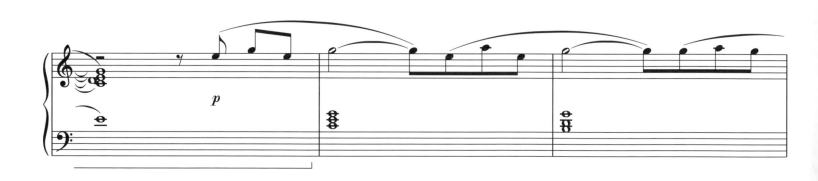

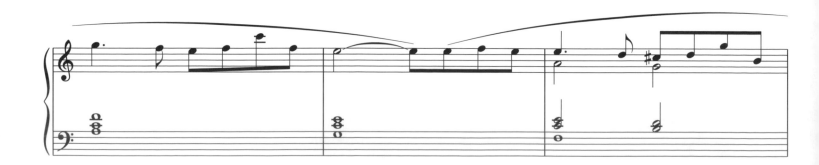

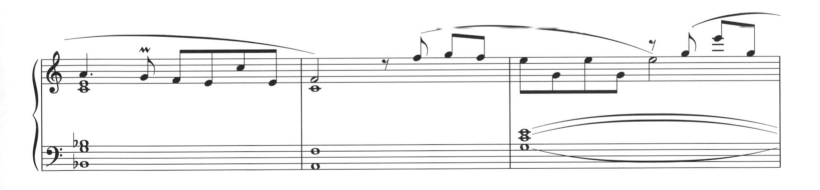

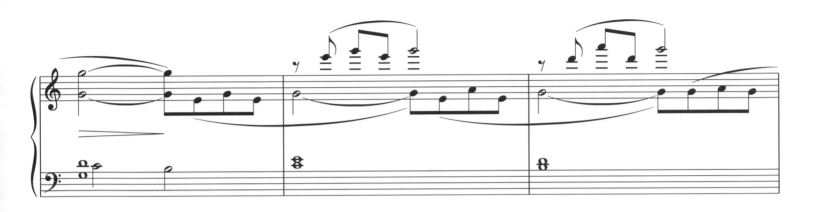

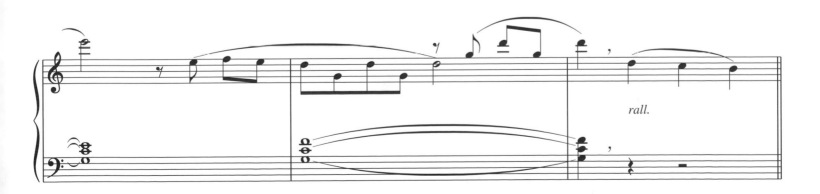

Mosso

A Tempo

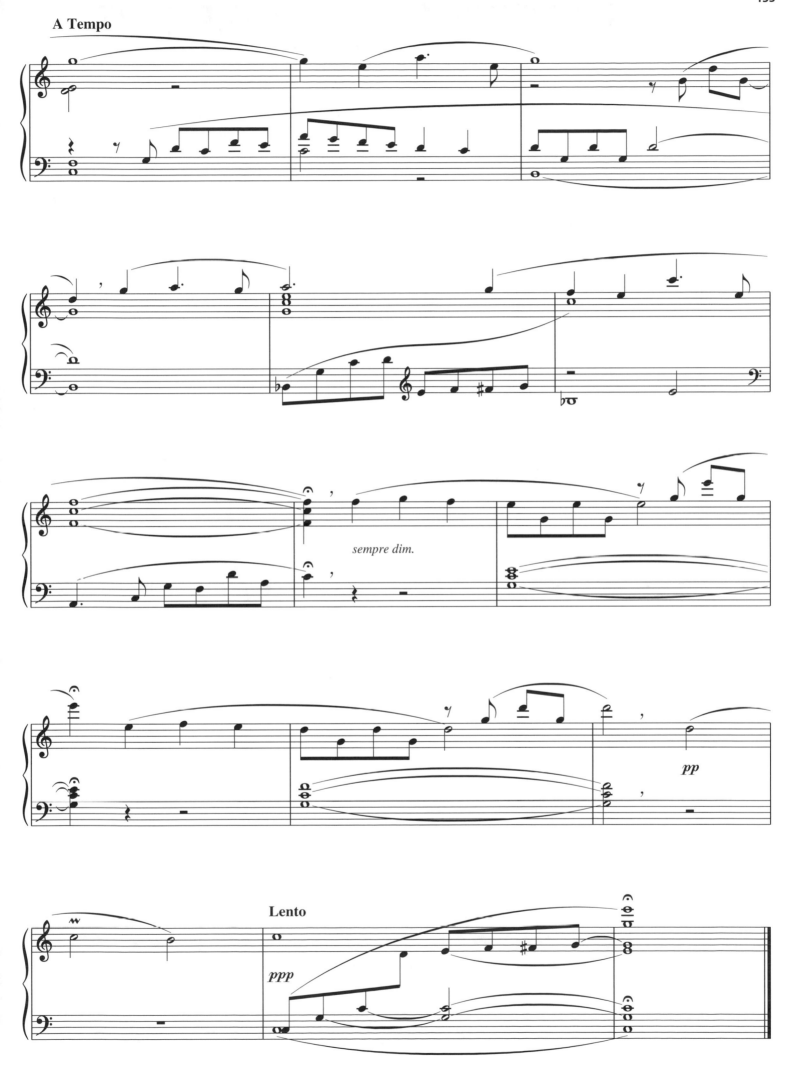

THE LAST TIME I FELT LIKE THIS

from SAME TIME, NEXT YEAR

Words by ALAN BERGMAN and MARILYN BERGMAN
Music by MARVIN HAMLISCH

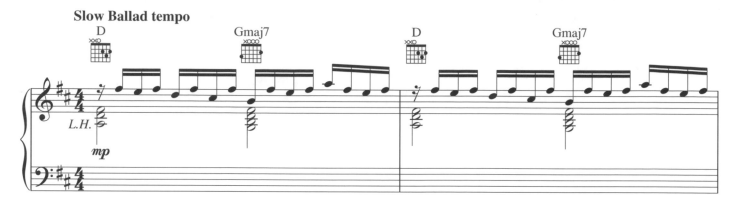

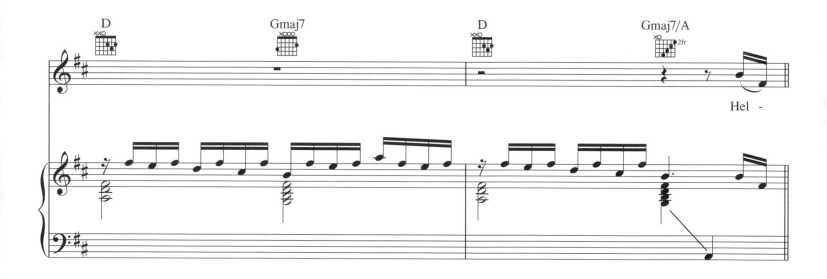

Hel -

lo,   I don't_ e - ven know_ your name,   but I'm hop - in' all __ the
lo,   I can't_ wait till we're a - lone,   some-where qui - et on __ our

135

LEGENDS OF THE FALL

from TriStar Pictures' LEGENDS OF THE FALL

Composed by JAMES HORNER

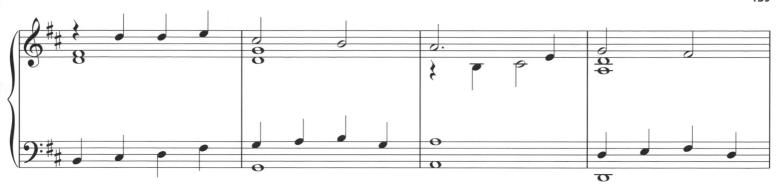

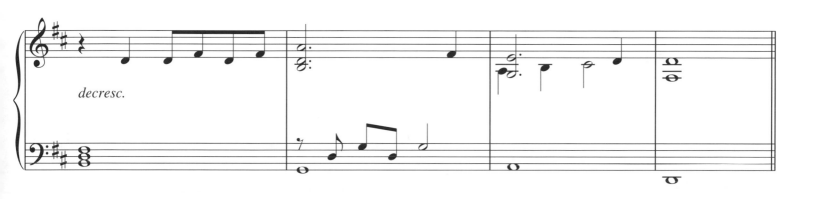

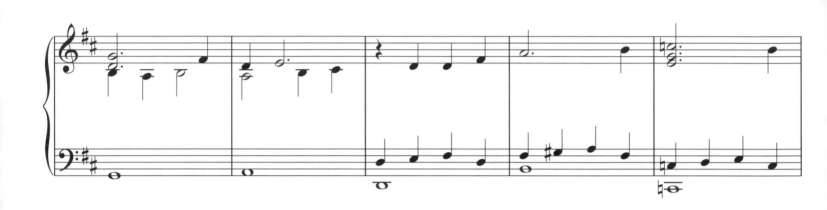

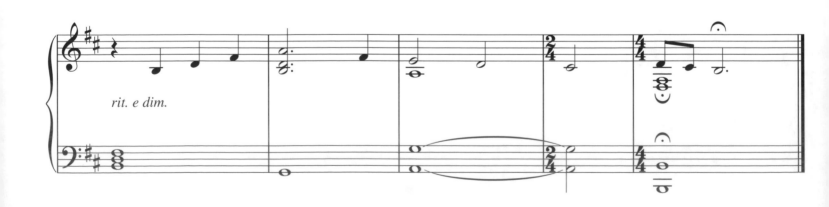

MIDNIGHT COWBOY
from the Motion Picture MIDNIGHT COWBOY

Music by JOHN BARRY
Lyric by JACK GOLD

Moderately slow

(Mid-night Cow-boy, Mid-night Cow-boy, see the lone-some Mid-night Cow-boy.)

Once _____ his hopes were high _____ as the sky, once _____ a dream was

LET THE RIVER RUN

Theme from the Motion Picture WORKING GIRL

Words and Music by
CARLY SIMON

LOVE ME TENDER
from LOVE ME TENDER

Words and Music by ELVIS PRESLEY
and VERA MATSON

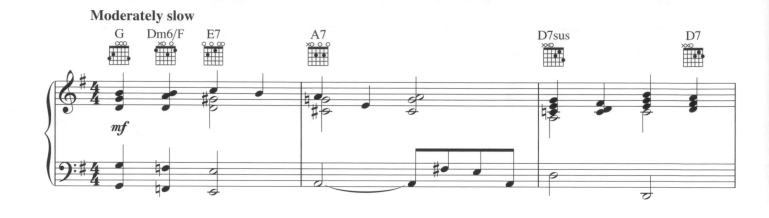

Love me ten - der, love me sweet,
Love me ten - der, love me long,
Love me ten - der, love me dear,
When at last my dreams come true,

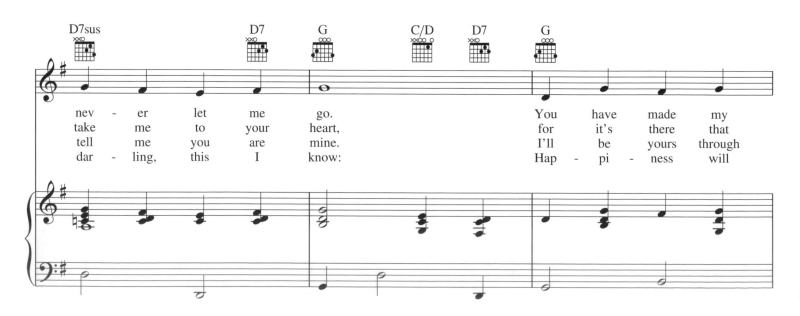

nev - er let me go.
take me to your heart,
tell me you are mine.
dar - ling, this I know:

You have made my
for it's there that
I'll be yours through
Hap - pi - ness will

THE MAN FROM SNOWY RIVER

(Main Title Theme)

from THE MAN FROM SNOWY RIVER

By BRUCE ROWLAND

Moderately

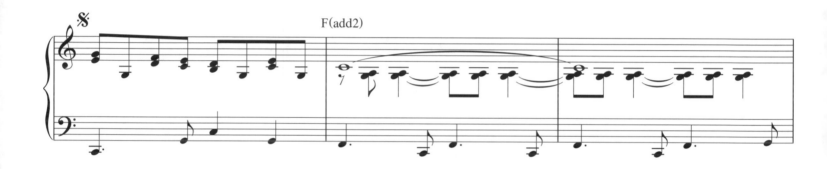

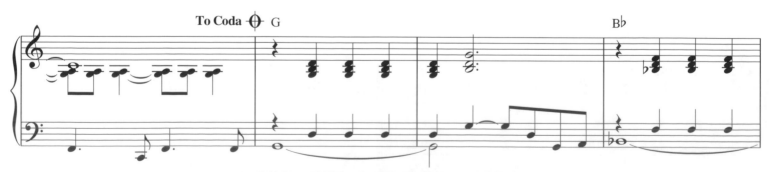

MOON RIVER
from the Paramount Picture BREAKFAST AT TIFFANY'S

Words by JOHNNY MERCER
Music by HENRY MANCINI

THE NEARNESS OF YOU

from the Paramount Picture ROMANCE IN THE DARK

Words by NED WASHINGTON
Music by HOAGY CARMICHAEL

NINE TO FIVE

from NINE TO FIVE

Words and Music by
DOLLY PARTON

Tum- ble out of bed and stum- ble to the kitch- en; pour my- self a cup ___
They let you dream just to watch them shat- ter; you're just a step on

___ of am- bi- tion, and yawn, and stretch, and try to come ___ to life. ___
the boss man's lad- der, but you've got dreams he'll nev- er take ___ a- way. ___

Jump in the show- er, and the blood starts pump- ing;
In the same boat with a lot of your friends,

NO TWO PEOPLE

from the Motion Picture HANS CHRISTIAN ANDERSEN

By FRANK LOESSER

ON GOLDEN POND
Main Theme from ON GOLDEN POND

Music by DAVE GRUSIN

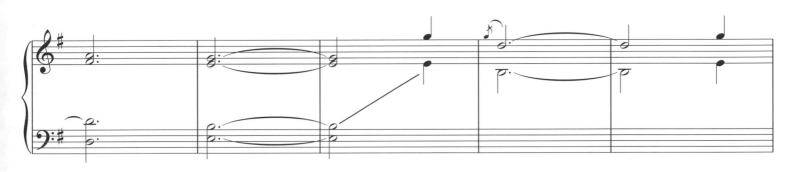

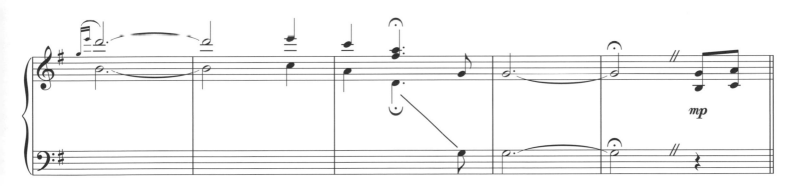

Andante rubato

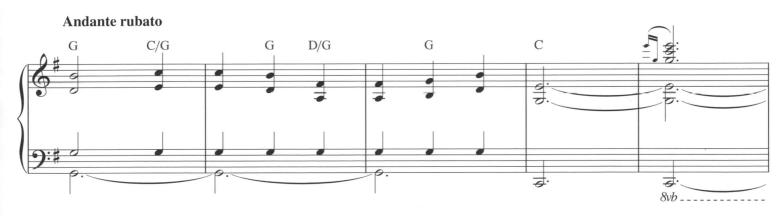

THE ODD COUPLE
Theme from the Paramount Picture THE ODD COUPLE

Words by SAMMY CAHN
Music by NEAL HEFTI

No mat - ter where they go, _____ they are known as the cou - ple. _____ They're nev - er seen a - lone, _____ so they're known as the cou - ple. _____

ONE TIN SOLDIER

from BILLY JACK

Words and Music by DENNIS LAMBERT
and BRIAN POTTER

182

Jus - ti - fy it in the end. ___ There won't be an - y trum-pets blow - in' ___

come the judge - ment day. On the blood - y morn - ing af - ter ___

___ one tin sol - dier rides a - way. ___

THEME FROM "ORDINARY PEOPLE"

Arranged by MARVIN HAMLISCH

Sostenuto (♪ = ca. 100)

Peo - ple. _____

I HAD A FARM IN AFRICA
(Main Title)
from OUT OF AFRICA

Music by JOHN BARRY

Moderately slow

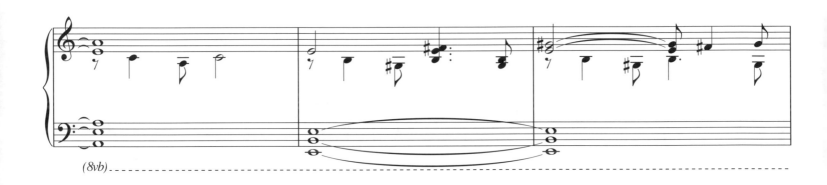

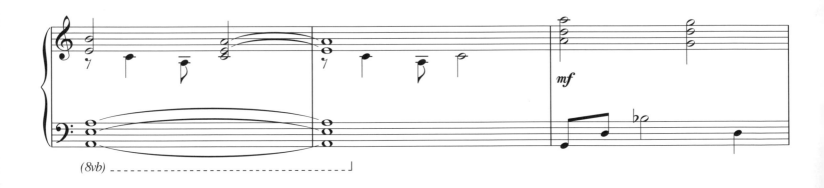

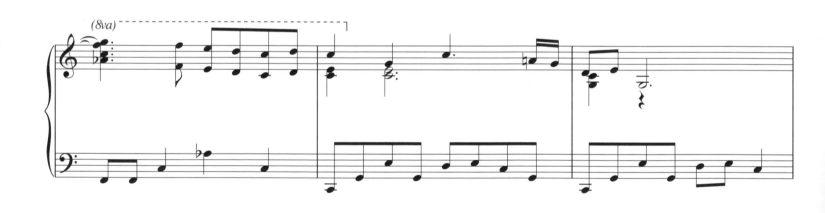

THE RAINBOW CONNECTION

from THE MUPPET MOVIE

Words and Music by PAUL WILLIAMS
and KENNETH L. ASCHER

Why are there so man-y songs a-bout rain-bows, and
Who said that ev-'ry wish would be heard and an-swered when

what's on the oth - er side? _____
wished on the morn - ing star? _____

Rain - bows are vi - sions, ___ but on - ly il - lu - sions, and
Some - bod - y thought of that, and some - one be - lieved it;

RAINDROPS KEEP FALLIN' ON MY HEAD

from BUTCH CASSIDY AND THE SUNDANCE KID

Lyric by HAL DAVID
Music by BURT BACHARACH

Rhythmically

Rain - drops keep fall - in' on my head, and just like the guy whose feet are too big for his bed, noth - in' seems to fit. Those rain - drops are fall - in' on my head. They keep fall - in'. So I just did me some talk - in' to the

SAY YOU, SAY ME

from the Motion Picture WHITE NIGHTS

Words and Music by
LIONEL RICHIE

Slow Ballad

mp

Say you, — say me. — Say it for al-

- ways. That's the way it should be. — Say you, — say me. —

— Say it to-geth - er, nat - 'ral - ly. —

Tempo I

lieve in who ___ you are; ___ you are a shin - ing star. ___

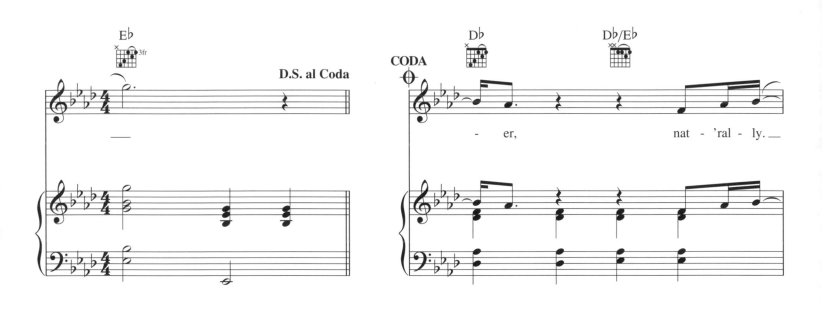

D.S. al Coda

CODA

___ - er, nat - 'ral - ly. ___

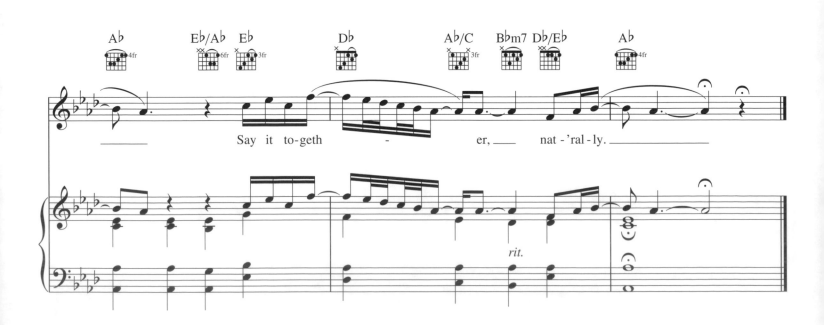

Say it to-geth - er, ___ nat - 'ral - ly. ___

rit.

SEASONS OF LOVE

from RENT

Words and Music by
JONATHAN LARSON

THEME FROM "SCHINDLER'S LIST"

from the Universal Motion Picture SCHINDLER'S LIST

Composed by JOHN WILLIAMS

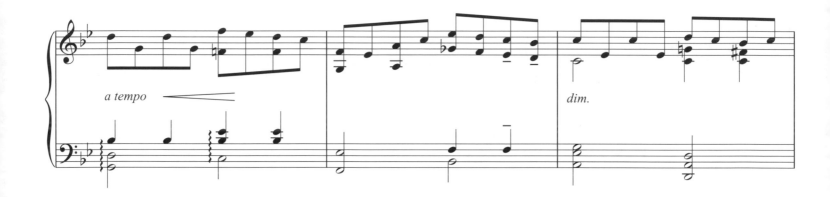

SEA OF LOVE
featured in the Motion Picture SEA OF LOVE

Words and Music by GEORGE KHOURY
and PHILIP BAPTISTE

THEME FROM SHAFT

from SHAFT

Words and Music by
ISAAC HAYES

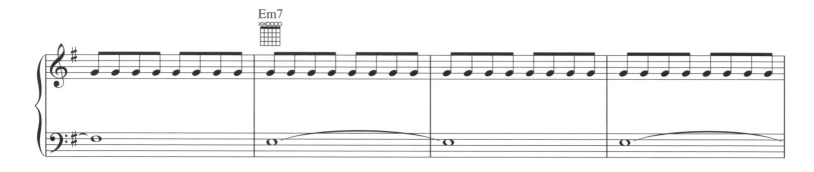

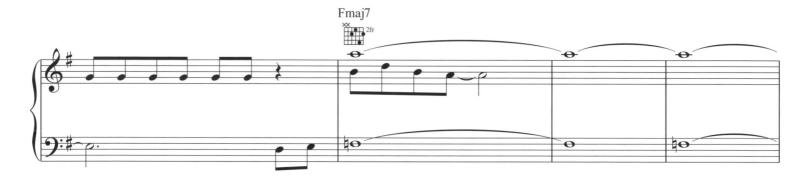

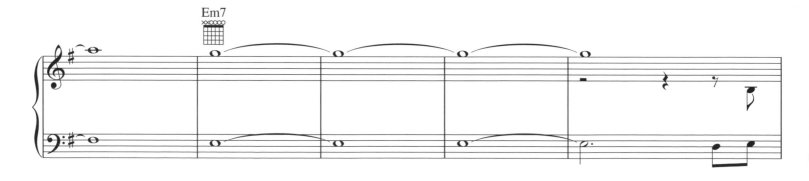

(Spoken:) Who's the black pri - vate dick ___ that's a sex ma - chine to all the chicks?   (Shaft!)

You're damn right!

Who   is the man that would risk his life for his broth - er man? _   (Shaft!)

no one un-der-stands him but his wom-an. (John Shaft!)

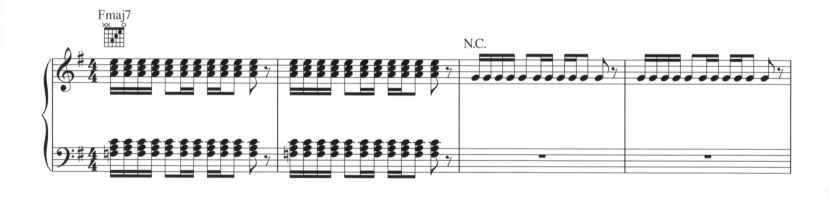

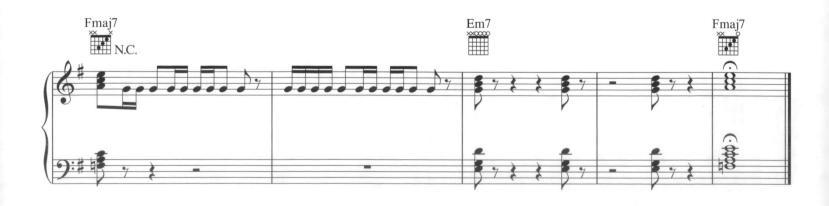

SOMEWHERE, MY LOVE
Lara's Theme from DOCTOR ZHIVAGO

Lyric by PAUL FRANCIS WEBSTER
Music by MAURICE JARRE

Some - where, my love, there will be songs to sing,

al - though the snow cov - ers the hope of spring.

Some - where a hill blos-soms in green and gold,

SOMEWHERE IN TIME
from SOMEWHERE IN TIME

Words by B.A. ROBERTSON
Music by JOHN BARRY

A SPOONFUL OF SUGAR

from Walt Disney's MARY POPPINS

Words and Music by RICHARD M. SHERMAN
and ROBERT B. SHERMAN

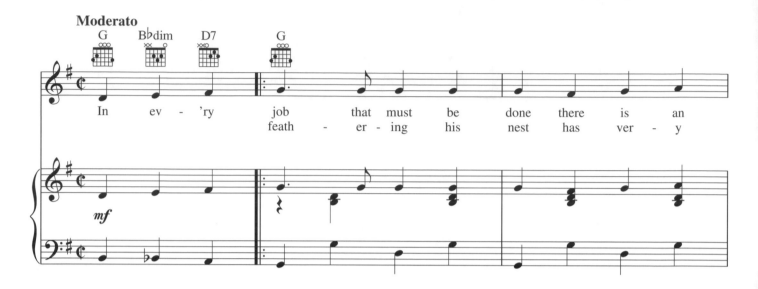

take — — — — be - comes a piece of cake, a lark! A
suit, he has a mer - ry tune to toot; he knows a

spree! It's ver - y clear to see that a
song will move the job a - long for a

spoon - ful of sug - ar helps the med - i - cine go

STAYIN' ALIVE
from the Motion Picture SATURDAY NIGHT FEVER

Words and Music by BARRY GIBB,
ROBIN GIBB and MAURICE GIBB

Medium Rock beat

Well, you can tell

by the way I use my walk, I'm a wom-an's man: no time to talk.

get low and I get high, and if I can't get ei-ther, I real-ly try. Got the

Mu-sic loud and wom-en warm, I've been kicked a-round since I was born. And now it's

wings of heav-en on my shoes. I'm a danc-in' man and I just can't lose. You know it's

Life go - in' no - where. _____ Some - bod - y help me. _____

Some - bod - y help _ me, yeah. _____

Life go- in' no - where. _____ Some - bod - y help _ me, yeah. _____ I'm stay- in' a - live. _

Repeat and Fade

LOVE THEME FROM "ST. ELMO'S FIRE"

from the Motion Picture ST. ELMO'S FIRE

Words and Music by
DAVID FOSTER

STORMY WEATHER
(Keeps Rainin' All the Time)
featured in the Motion Picture STORMY WEATHER

Lyric by TED KOEHLER
Music by HAROLD ARLEN

Interlude

THE STRIPPER
from THE STRIPPER

Music by DAVID ROSE

Blues tempo

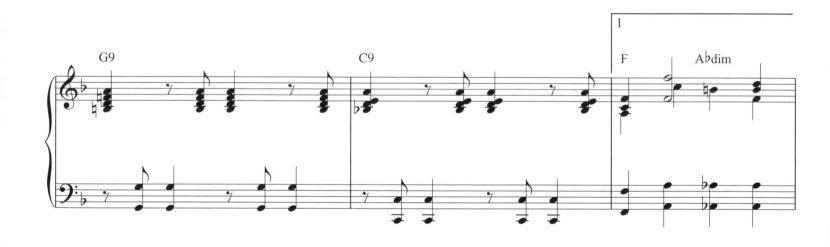

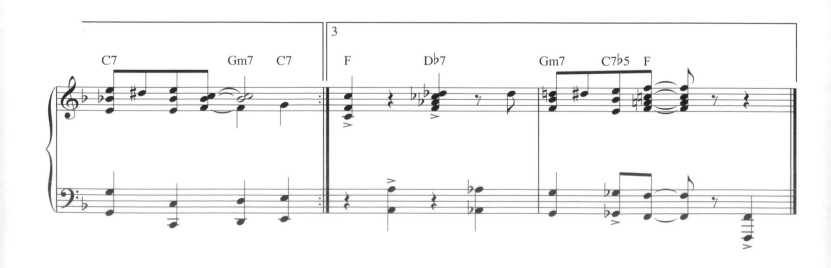

TEACHER'S PET

from TEACHER'S PET

Words and Music by
JOE LUBIN

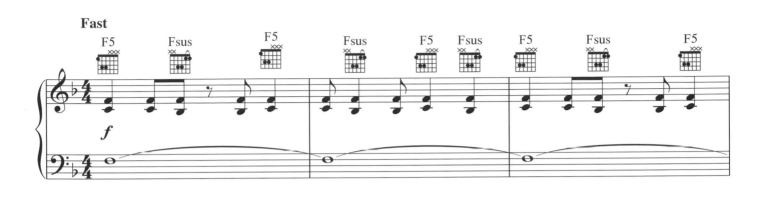

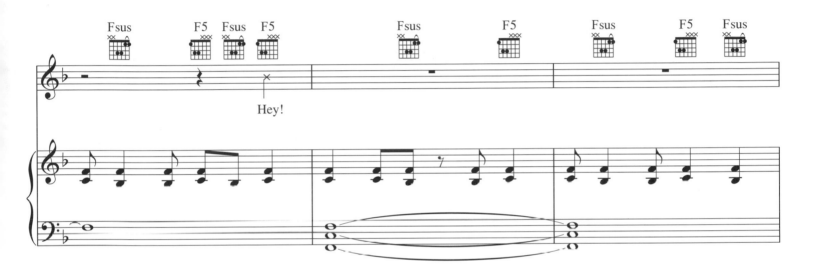

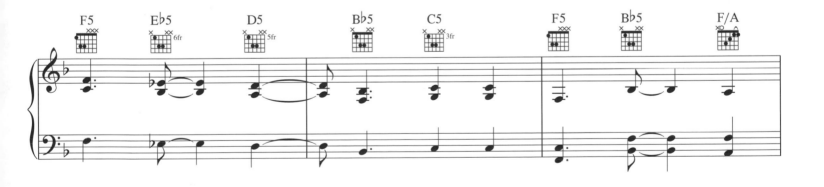

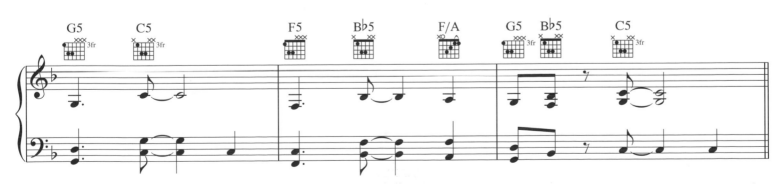

248

TAMMY
from TAMMY AND THE BACHELOR

Words and Music by JAY LIVINGSTON
and RAY EVANS

TAXI DRIVER
(Theme)
from TAXI DRIVER

By BERNARD HERRMANN

Rubato, espressivo (slow feeling)

THEME FROM "TERMS OF ENDEARMENT"

from the Paramount Picture TERMS OF ENDEARMENT

By MICHAEL GORE

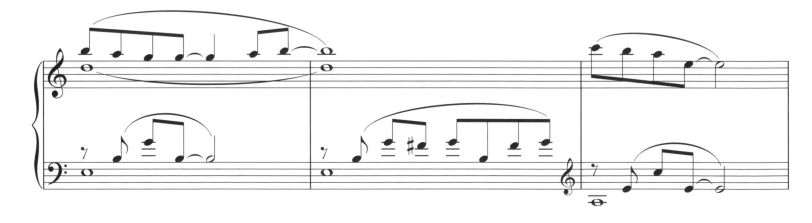

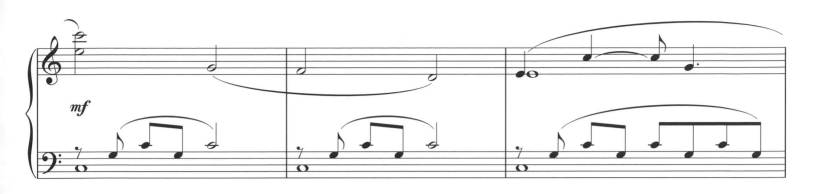

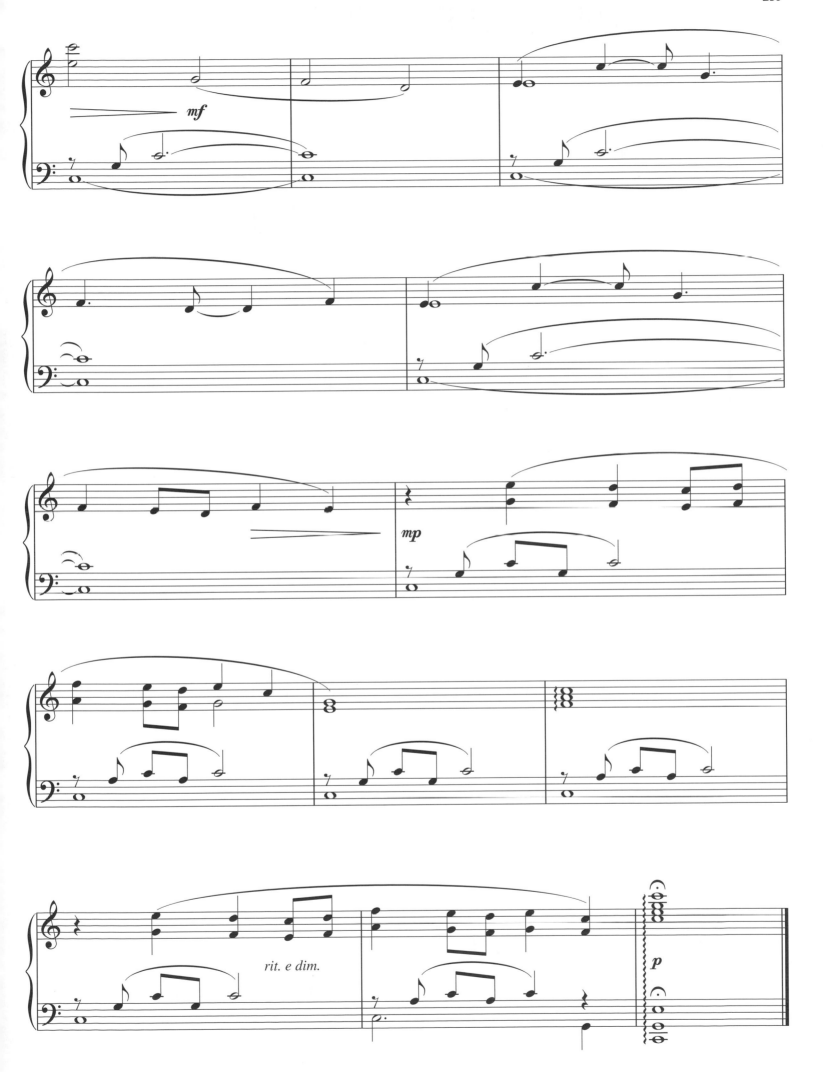

THAT THING YOU DO!

from the Original Motion Picture Soundtrack THAT THING YOU DO!

Words and Music by
ADAM SCHLESINGER

(I've Had)
THE TIME OF MY LIFE
from DIRTY DANCING

Words and Music by FRANKE PREVITE,
JOHN DeNICOLA and DONALD MARKOWITZ

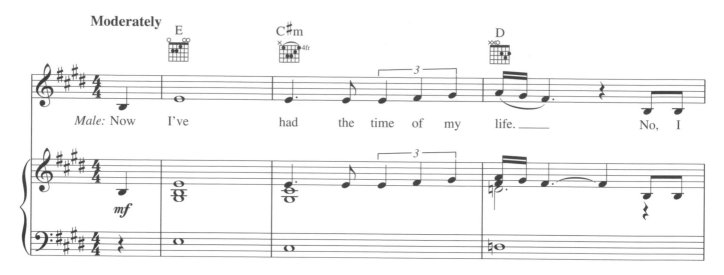

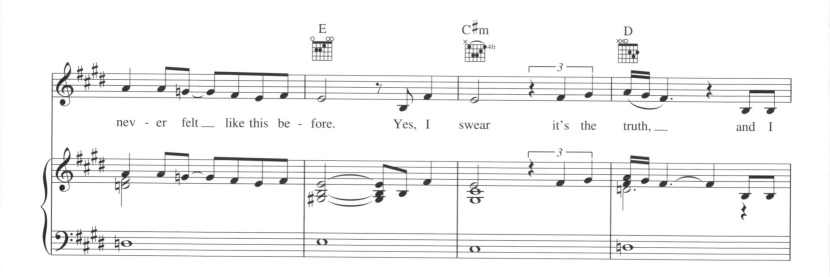

E

sy. _____

Both: Now with

D/E

pas - sion in our eyes _____ there's no way we could _ dis - guise _____ it se - cret -

E

ly. _____

So we

D/E

take each oth - er's hand _____ 'cause we seem to un - der - stand _ the ur - gen -

just let it go;___ don't be a - fraid to lose con - trol.___

Female: Yes, I know what's on ___ your mind when you say stay with me to-

night. ___ *Male:* Stay ___ with me. Just re - mem - ber, you're the

one thing ___ *Female:* I ___ can't get e - nough of. *Male:* So I'll tell you

TO SIR, WITH LOVE

from TO SIR, WITH LOVE

Words by DON BLACK
Music by MARC LONDON

Moderately

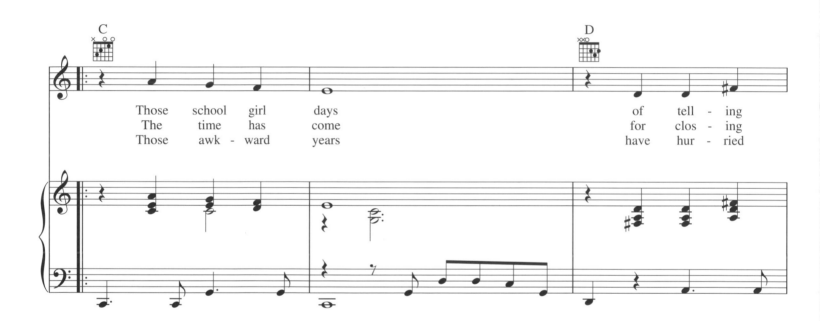

Those   school   girl   days   of   tell - ing
The   time   has   come   for   clos - ing
Those   awk - ward   years   have   hur - ried

tales   and   bit - ing   nails   are   gone, _____
books,   and   long   last   looks   must   end. _____
by.   Why   did   they   fly   a - way? _____

TOP HAT, WHITE TIE AND TAILS

from the RKO Radio Motion Picture TOP HAT

Words and Music by
IRVING BERLIN

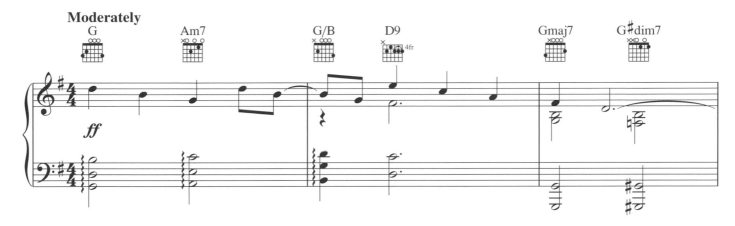

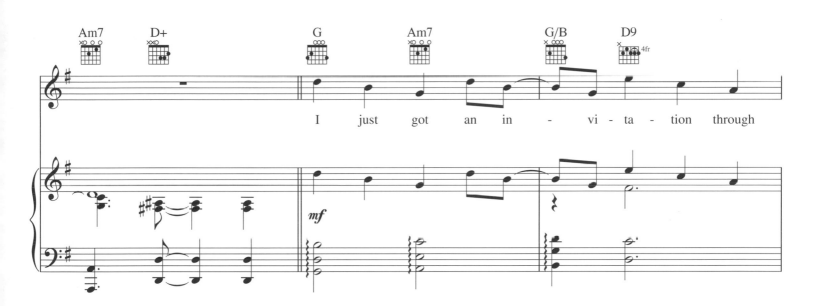

I just got an in - vi - ta - tion through

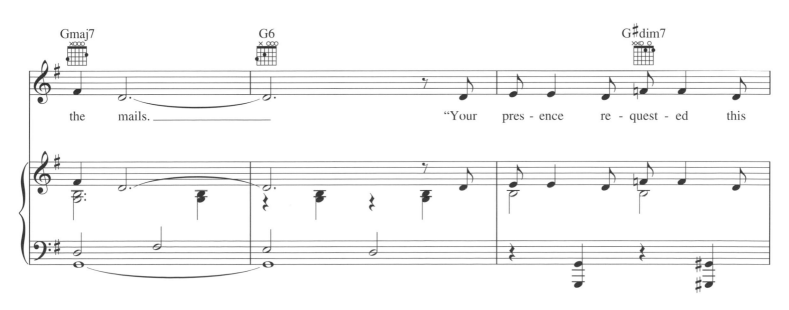

the mails. _____ "Your pres - ence re - quest - ed this

279

VIVA LAS VEGAS

from VIVA LAS VEGAS

Words and Music by DOC POMUS
and MORT SHUMAN

Lyrics:

Bright light cit - y gon - na
how I wish that
keep on the run. I'm gon - na

set my soul, __ gon - na set my soul __ on __ fire. __ There's a
there were more __ than twen - ty - four hours __ in the day. __ But
have me some fun if it costs me my ver - y last __ dime. __ If I

whole lot of mon-ey that's _ read-y to burn, _ so get those stakes _ up _
e-ven if _ there were _ for-ty _ more _ I would-n't sleep a min-ute a-way. _
wind up _ broke _ then I'll al-ways re-mem-ber that I had _ a swing-in' time.

high-er. There's a thou-sand pret-ty wom-en just wait-in' out there. _
Oh, there's black-jack, po-ker and a rou-lette _ wheel, _ a
I'm gon-na give it ev-'ry-thing I _ got. _

They're all _ liv-in' dev-il may care, _ and I'm just a dev-il with
for-tune won and lost on _ ev-er-y deal. _ All you need's a strong heart and a
La-dy Luck, _ please let the dice _ stay hot. _ Let me shoot a sev-en with

Guitar solo

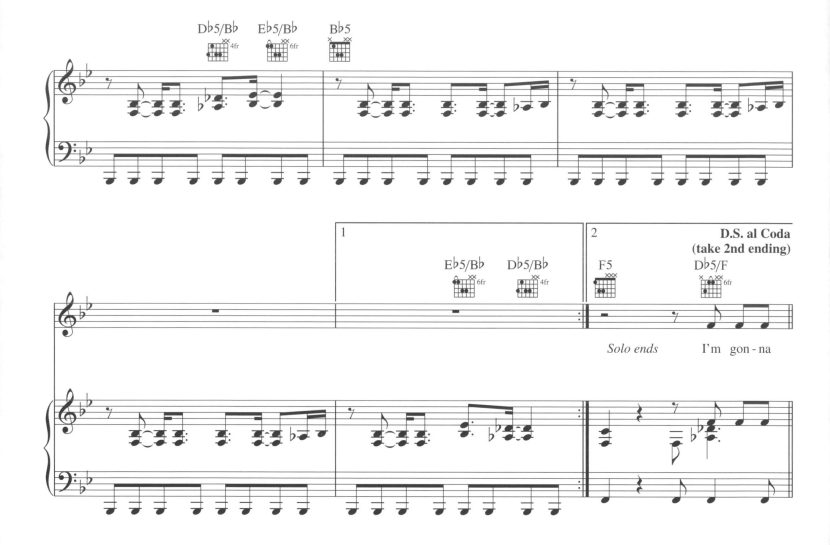

Solo ends   I'm gon-na

D.S. al Coda
(take 2nd ending)

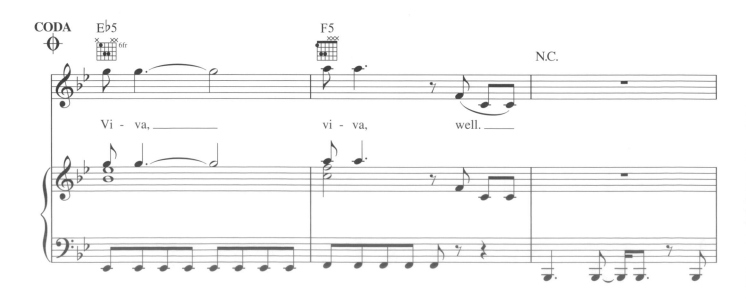

Vi - va, _____   vi - va,   well. _____

THE WAY WE WERE

from the Motion Picture THE WAY WE WERE

Words by ALAN and MARILYN BERGMAN
Music by MARVIN HAMLISCH

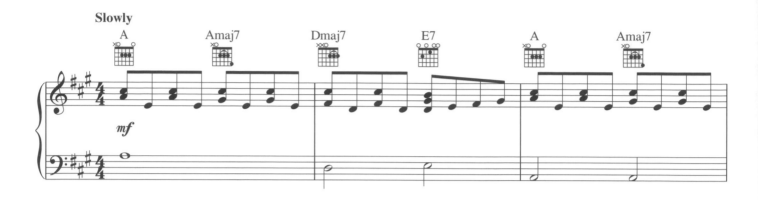

Mem - 'ries _____ light the cor - ners of my
pic - tures _____ of the smiles we left be -
Mem - 'ries _____ may be beau - ti - ful, and

mind.
hind, Mist - y wa - ter - col - or mem - 'ries _____
yet, smiles we gave to one an - oth - er _____
what's too pain - ful to re - mem - ber _____

To Coda ⊕

WHEN I FALL IN LOVE

featured in the TriStar Motion Picture SLEEPLESS IN SEATTLE

Words by EDWARD HEYMAN
Music by VICTOR YOUNG

Slowly, with much feeling

When I fall in love

it will be for-ev-er, or I'll nev-er

fall in love. In a

WHERE IS YOUR HEART
(The Song from Moulin Rouge)
from MOULIN ROUGE

Words by WILLIAM ENGVICK
Music by GEORGE AURIC

YOU MUST LOVE ME

from the Cinergi Motion Picture EVITA

Words by TIM RICE
Music by ANDREW LLOYD WEBBER

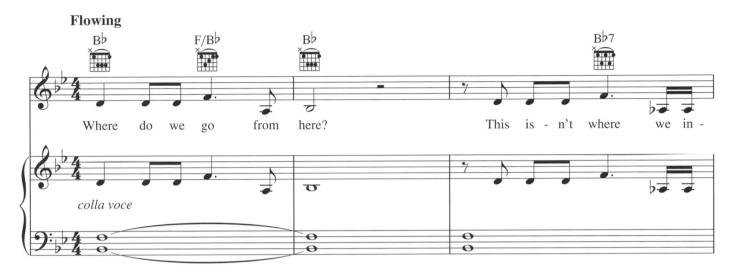

Where do we go from here? This is-n't where we in-

tend-ed to be. We had it all, you be-lieved in me, I be-

lieved in you. Cer-tain-ties dis-ap-
Why are you at my

YOUNG AT HEART

from YOUNG AT HEART

Words by CAROLYN LEIGH
Music by JOHNNY RICHARDS

Fair-y tales ___ can come true, ___ it can hap-pen to you ___ if you're young at heart. ___ For it's hard ___ you will find, ___ to be nar-row of mind ___ if you're young at heart. ___ You can

THE ULTIMATE SERIES

This comprehensive series features jumbo collections of piano/vocal arrangements with guitar chords. Each volume features an outstanding selection of your favorite songs. Collect them all for the ultimate music library!

Blues

90 blues classics, including: Boom Boom • Born Under a Bad Sign • Gee Baby, Ain't I Good to You • I Can't Quit You Baby • Pride and Joy • (They Call It) Stormy Monday • Sweet Home Chicago • Why I Sing the Blues • You Shook Me • and more.
00310723 . . . .$19.95

Broadway Gold

100 show tunes: Beauty and the Beast • Do-Re-Mi • I Whistle a Happy Tune • The Lady Is a Tramp • Memory • My Funny Valentine • Oklahoma • Some Enchanted Evening • Summer Nights • Tomorrow • many more.
00361396 . . . .$21.95

Broadway Platinum

100 popular Broadway show tunes, featuring: Consider Yourself • Getting to Know You • Gigi • Do You Hear the People Sing • I'll Be Seeing You • My Favorite Things • People • She Loves Me • Try to Remember • Younger Than Springtime • many more.
00311496 . . . .$19.95

Children's Songbook

66 fun songs for kids: Alphabet Song • Be Our Guest • Bingo • The Brady Bunch • Do-Re-Mi • Hakuna Matata • It's a Small World • Kum Ba Yah • Sesame Street Theme • Tomorrow • Won't You Be My Neighbor? • and more.
00310690 . . . .$18.95

Christmas – Third Edition

Includes: Carol of the Bells • Deck the Hall • Frosty the Snow Man • Gesu Bambino • Good King Wenceslas • Jingle-Bell Rock • Joy to the World • Nuttin' for Christmas • O Holy Night • Rudolph the Red-Nosed Reindeer • Silent Night • What Child Is This? • and more.
00361399 . . . .$19.95

Classic Rock

70 rock classics in one great collection! Includes: Angie • Best of My Love • California Girls • Crazy Little Thing Called Love • I Love Rock'N'Roll • Joy to the World • Landslide • Light My Fire • Livin' on a Prayer • Mony, Mony • (She's) Some Kind of Wonderful • Sultans of Swing • Sweet Emotion • Werewolves of London • Wonderful Tonight • Ziggy Stardust • and more.
00310962 . . . .$22.95

Country – Second Edition

90 of your favorite country hits: Boot Scootin' Boogie • Chattahoochie • Could I Have This Dance • Crazy • Down at the Twist And Shout • Hey, Good Lookin' • Lucille • When She Cries • and more.
00310036 . . . .$19.95

Early Rock 'N' Roll

100 classics, including: All Shook Up • Bye Bye Love • Duke of Earl • Gloria • Hello Mary Lou • It's My Party • Johnny B. Goode • The Loco-Motion • Lollipop • Surfin' U.S.A. • The Twist • Wooly Bully • Yakety Yak • and more.
00361411 . . . .$21.95

Gospel

Includes: El Shaddai • His Eye Is on the Sparrow • How Great Thou Art • Just a Closer Walk With Thee • Lead Me, Guide Me • (There'll Be) Peace in the Valley (For Me) • Precious Lord, Take My Hand • Wings of a Dove • more.
00241009 . . . .$19.95

Jazz Standards

Over 100 great jazz favorites: Ain't Misbehavin' • All of Me • Come Rain or Come Shine • Here's That Rainy Day • I'll Take Romance • Imagination • Li'l Darlin' • Manhattan • Moonglow • Moonlight in Vermont • A Night in Tunisia • The Party's Over • Solitude • Star Dust • and more.
00361407 . . . .$19.95

Latin Songs

80 hot Latin favorites, including: Amapola (Pretty Little Poppy) • Amor • Bésame Mucho (Kiss Me Much) • Blame It on the Bossa Nova • Feelings (¿Dime?) • Malagueña • Mambo No. 5 • Perfidia • Slightly out of Tune (Desafinado) • What a Diff'rence a Day Made • more.
00310689 . . . .$19.95

Love and Wedding Songbook

90 songs of devotion including: The Anniversary Waltz • Canon in D • Endless Love • Forever and Ever, Amen • Just the Way You Are • Love Me Tender • Sunrise, Sunset • Through the Years • Trumpet Voluntary • and more!
00361445 . . . .$19.95

Movie Music

73 favorites from the big screen, including: Can You Feel the Love Tonight • Chariots of Fire • Cruella De Vil • Driving Miss Daisy • Easter Parade • Forrest Gump • Moon River • That Thing You Do! • Viva Las Vegas • The Way We Were • When I Fall in Love • and more.
00310240 . . . .$18.95

FOR MORE INFORMATION, SEE YOUR LOCAL MUSIC DEALER, OR WRITE TO:

HAL•LEONARD®
CORPORATION
7777 W. BLUEMOUND RD. P.O. BOX 13819 MILWAUKEE, WI 53213

http://www.halleonard.com
Prices, contents, and availability subject to change without notice.
Availability and pricing may vary outside the U.S.A.

Nostalgia Songs

100 great favorites from yesteryear, such as: Ain't We Got Fun? • Alexander's Ragtime Band • Casey Jones • Chicago • Danny Boy • Second Hand Rose • Swanee • Toot, Toot, Tootsie! • 'Way Down Yonder in New Orleans • The Yellow Rose of Texas • You Made Me Love You • and more!
00310730 . . . .$17.95

Pop/Rock

70 of the most popular pop/rock hits of our time, including: Bad, Bad Leroy Brown • Bohemian Rhapsody • Complicated • Drops of Jupiter (Tell Me) • Dust in the Wind • Every Little Thing She Does Is Magic • (Everything I Do) I Do It for You • From a Distance • I Don't Want to Wait • I Will Remember You • Imagine • Invisible Touch • More Than Words • Smooth • Tears in Heaven • Thriller • Walking in Memphis • You Are So Beautiful • and more.
00310963 . . . .$22.95

Singalong!

100 of the best-loved popular songs ever: Beer Barrel Polka • Crying in the Chapel • Edelweiss • Feelings • Five Foot Two, Eyes of Blue • For Me and My Gal • Indiana • It's a Small World • Que Sera, Sera • This Land Is Your Land • When Irish Eyes Are Smiling • and more.
00361418 . . . .$18.95

Standard Ballads

91 mellow masterpieces, including: Angel Eyes • Body and Soul • Darn That Dream • Day By Day • Easy to Love • Isn't It Romantic? • Misty • Mona Lisa • Moon River • My Funny Valentine • Smoke Gets in Your Eyes • When I Fall in Love • and more.
00310246 . . . .$19.95

Swing Standards

93 songs to get you swinging, including: Bandstand Boogie • Boogie Woogie Bugle Boy • Heart and Soul • How High the Moon • In the Mood • Moonglow • Satin Doll • Sentimental Journey • Witchcraft • and more.
00310245 . . . .$19.95

TV Themes

More than 90 themes from your favorite TV show including: The Addams Family Theme • Cleveland Roc Theme from Frasier • Happy Days • Love Boat T Hey, Hey We're the Monkees • Nadia's Theme Street Theme • Theme from Star Trek® • and m
00310841 . . . .